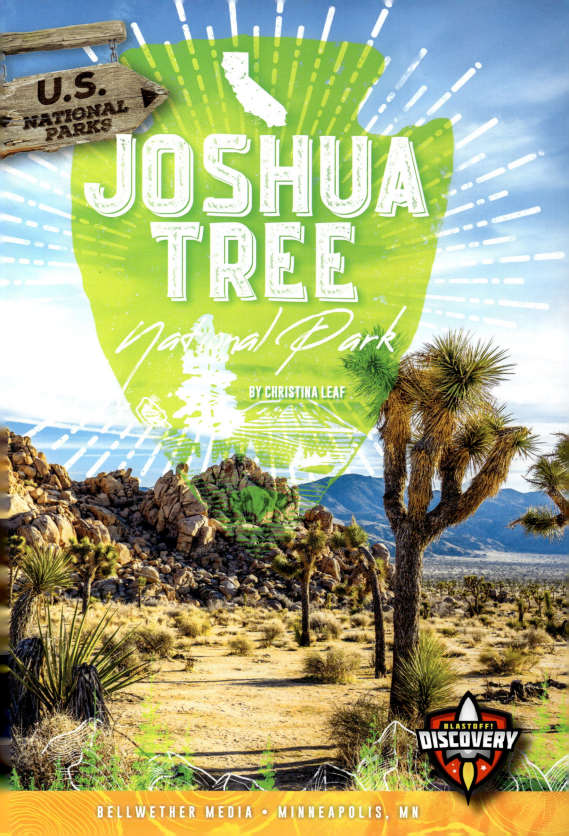

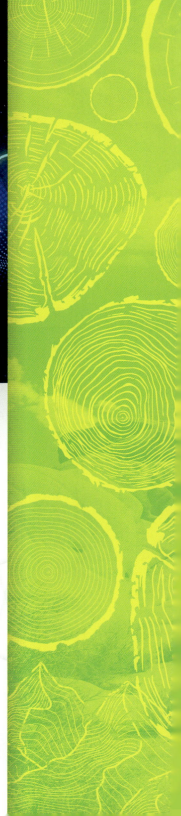

This edition first published in 2024 by Bellwether Media, Inc.

No part of this publication may be reproduced in whole or in part without written permission of the publisher.
For information regarding permission, write to Bellwether Media, Inc., Attention: Permissions Department,
6012 Blue Circle Drive, Minnetonka, MN 55343.

Library of Congress Cataloging-in-Publication Data

Names: Leaf, Christina, author.
Title: Joshua Tree National Park / by Christina Leaf.
Other titles: Blastoff! discovery. U.S. National Parks.
Description: Minneapolis, MN : Bellwether Media, Inc., 2024. | Series: Blastoff! discovery : U.S. national parks | Includes bibliographical references and index. | Audience: Ages 7-13 | Audience: Grades 4-6 | Summary: "Engaging images accompany information about Joshua Tree National Park. The combination of high-interest subject matter and narrative text is intended for students in grades 3 through 8" – Provided by publisher.
Identifiers: LCCN 2023045251 (print) | LCCN 2023045252 (ebook) | ISBN 9798886878141 (library binding) | ISBN 9798886879087 (ebook)
Subjects: LCSH: Joshua Tree National Park (Calif.)–Juvenile literature. | CYAC: National parks and reserves | Joshua Tree National Park (Calif.)
Classification: LCC F868.J6+ (print) | LCC F868.J6+ (ebook) | DDC 979.497–dc23/eng/20231006
LC record available at https://lccn.loc.gov/2023045251
LC ebook record available at https://lccn.loc.gov/2023045252

Text copyright © 2024 by Bellwether Media, Inc. BLASTOFF! DISCOVERY and associated logos are trademarks and/or registered trademarks of Bellwether Media, Inc.

Editor: Rebecca Sabelko
Series Design: Jeffrey Kollock   Book Designer: Laura Sowers

Printed in the United States of America, North Mankato, MN.

TABLE OF CONTENTS

A Lost Oasis	4
Joshua Tree National Park	6
The Land	8
Plants and Wildlife	12
Humans in Joshua Tree National Park	16
Visiting Joshua Tree National Park	22
Protecting the Park	24
Joshua Tree National Park Facts	28
Glossary	30
To Learn More	31
Index	32

A LOST OASIS

BIGHORN SHEEP

It is a cool winter morning in Joshua Tree National Park. Two hikers set off toward the Lost Palms **Oasis**. The trail winds through sandy **washes**. Cacti and other plants dot the desert beyond the path.

LOST PALMS OASIS TRAIL

The hikers pass through a small **canyon**. Soon, they spy bighorn sheep climbing a rocky hill. The path leads the hikers down into another canyon. At the bottom, tall palm trees tower over them. They have reached a hidden oasis in the middle of the desert. Joshua Tree is full of secret wonders!

JOSHUA TREE NATIONAL PARK

Joshua Tree National Park is a unique area in southeastern California. Most of the park is desert. Two different deserts, the Mojave and the Colorado, lie within the park's boundaries. These two **ecosystems** give Joshua Tree a special blend of plants and animals. The park is named for the spiky Joshua trees that grow there. These trees only grow in a few other places in the world.

Joshua Tree covers 1,242 square miles (3,217 square kilometers). A number of cities lie just outside of the park. Palm Springs is the largest.

JOSHUA TREE

HOLY TREES

Stories say religious settlers named Joshua trees. The plants reminded the settlers of Joshua from the Bible, raising his arms in prayer.

THE LAND

Joshua Tree is part of a **rain shadow desert**. It lies on the eastern side of the Transverse Ranges. When storms blow inland from the Pacific Ocean, rain falls to the west of the mountains. The air is dry by the time it crosses the mountains.

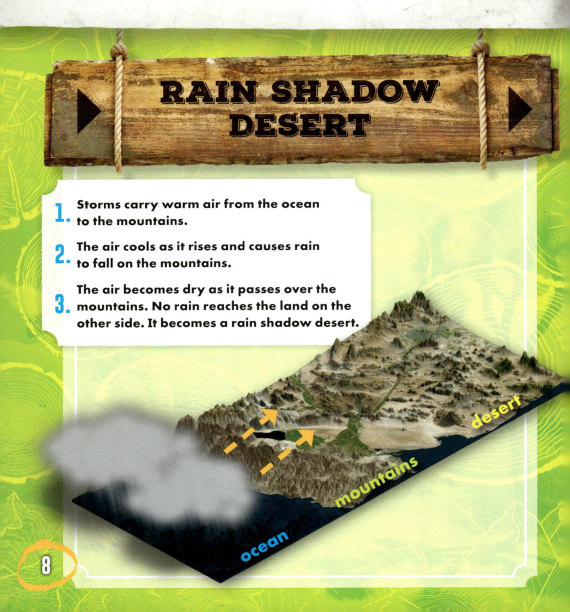

RAIN SHADOW DESERT

1. Storms carry warm air from the ocean to the mountains.
2. The air cools as it rises and causes rain to fall on the mountains.
3. The air becomes dry as it passes over the mountains. No rain reaches the land on the other side. It becomes a rain shadow desert.

MOJAVE DESERT

Joshua Tree is famous for its huge boulders. These formed more than 100 million years ago. **Magma** cooled underground and became rock. Over time, **erosion** wore away at the rocks. Water trickled down through spaces in the rock. This created large blocks and rounded their edges. Erosion also uncovered the boulders we see today!

Joshua Tree has a dry, varied landscape. The Colorado Desert covers the south and east. It is part of the larger Sonoran Desert. The western part of the park is part of the Mojave Desert. Small mountain ranges are scattered throughout the park. Woodland forests of juniper and pinyon pines cover their highest **elevations**.

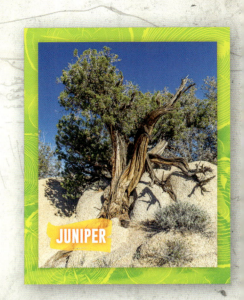

JUNIPER

   Joshua Tree can have extreme weather. But most days are clear and sunny. Only about 5 inches (13 centimeters) of rain fall each year. Summer brings high temperatures. Winter days are cool, while nights can dip below freezing. Snow may fall high in the mountains.

PLANTS AND WILDLIFE

Joshua trees grow throughout the park, though most are found in the Mojave Desert. They connect many of the park's animals. Orioles use their leaves to build nests in the trees. Yucca moths lay their eggs in Joshua tree flowers, and their young eat the seeds. The moths also pollinate the plants to keep them healthy.

Kangaroo rats and jackrabbits eat Joshua tree seeds. Ringtails and kit foxes hunt these small mammals for meals. Desert night lizards take shelter under fallen Joshua tree branches. Desert night snakes hunt the tiny lizards when the sun goes down.

SCOTT'S ORIOLE

KANGAROO RAT

KIT FOX

DESERT NIGHT LIZARD

BLACK-TAILED JACKRABBIT

FOOD FOR SLOTHS

Long ago, Joshua trees were an important food for giant sloths. These animals spread the trees' seeds. The trees grew in many more places!

JOSHUA TREE

Life Span: about 150 years
Status: least concern

Joshua tree range =

| LEAST CONCERN | NEAR THREATENED | VULNERABLE | ENDANGERED | CRITICALLY ENDANGERED | EXTINCT IN THE WILD | EXTINCT |

13

Cholla cacti rise from Joshua Tree's dry land. Horned lizards hide between rocks. Sidewinders slither across sand while burrowing owls find shelter underground. Rare rains cause bursts of colorful wildflowers. Oases of desert fan palms offer shade and homes for animals such as great horned owls and bats. Coyotes eat fruit from these tall trees.

CHOLLA CACTUS

DESERT HORNED LIZARD

Life Span: 5 to 8 years
Status: least concern

desert horned lizard range =

| LEAST CONCERN | NEAR THREATENED | VULNERABLE | ENDANGERED | CRITICALLY ENDANGERED | EXTINCT IN THE WILD | EXTINCT |

FROG AND TOAD

RED-SPOTTED TOAD

Two amphibians are found in the park. California treefrogs live near water sources. Red-spotted toads live mostly underground. They come out after rain falls.

MOJAVE ASTERS

In the park's mountains, bighorn sheep cross rocky peaks. Mountain lions hunt mule deer in the forests of juniper and pinyon pines. Purple Mojave asters add splashes of color to the forests. Life is everywhere in Joshua Tree!

HUMANS IN JOSHUA TREE NATIONAL PARK

Humans arrived in the area that is now Joshua Tree as early as 8,000 years ago. People of the **Pinto Culture** likely hunted large animals and gathered plants to eat. As the land changed, the Pinto people disappeared.

Later, the Serrano and the Cahuilla peoples made homes near sources of water. The Serrano lived in the north and the Cahuilla lived in the south. They used the land to find food and other **resources** when they were plentiful. The Chemehuevi people gathered food in certain seasons and later settled in the area. The Mojave people also occupied the area at different times.

Few Europeans visited the area until the mid-1800s. The United States took control of the land in 1848. By the late 1800s, the Serrano and the Chemehuevi struggled to keep their way of life.

More people were moving to southern California in the early 1900s. Cars and trains made visiting the desert easier. But visitors did not treat the land with care. They took desert plants for their gardens and burned Joshua trees.

SOUTHERN CALIFORNIA MINING STAGECOACH

KEYS RANCH

A man named Bill Keys lived in what is now Joshua Tree until 1969. He first worked for the gold mines and later raised cattle. Visitors can tour his ranch today.

19

MINERVA HOYT

A woman named Minerva Hoyt grew concerned about the damage to the desert. She worked hard to recommend the land for protection. In 1936, Hoyt's efforts paid off. President Franklin D. Roosevelt created Joshua Tree National Monument. Finally, in 1994 it became Joshua Tree National Park. The law added new land to the park, too.

Today, some Serrano, Cahuilla, and Chemehuevi people still live and work around the area. Around 3 million people visit Joshua Tree National Park each year. They come to experience the park's unique ecosystems. The park has even inspired artists to make music!

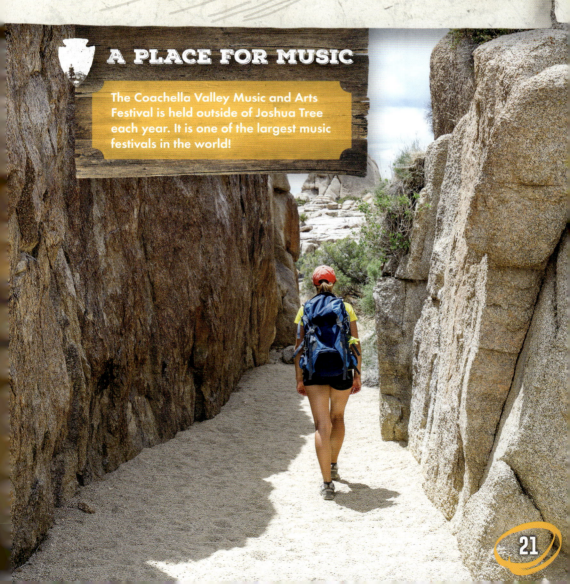

A PLACE FOR MUSIC

The Coachella Valley Music and Arts Festival is held outside of Joshua Tree each year. It is one of the largest music festivals in the world!

VISITING JOSHUA TREE NATIONAL PARK

There is plenty to do in Joshua Tree! The park's boulders are famous among rock climbers. Hikers trek through the desert landscape. People also ride horses or bicycles throughout the park. Bird-watchers search for speedy roadrunners and colorful visiting warblers. Those looking for adventure can take an off-roading tour.

ROCK CLIMBING

CAMPING

TOP SITES

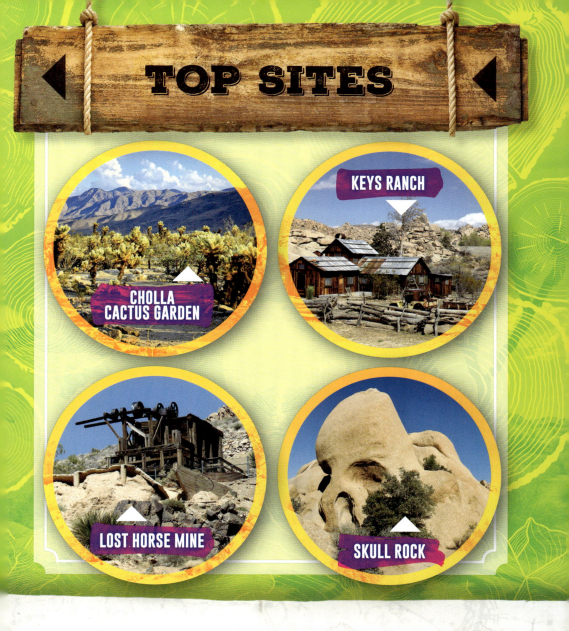

People set up tents among the park's giant boulders and camp in the desert. Stargazers take in the park's dark skies. Some may even come for October's Night Sky Festival. Other people visit in spring to see wildflowers carpet the desert!

PROTECTING THE PARK

Climate change is the biggest threat Joshua Tree faces today. This human-caused **phenomenon** makes the park hotter and drier. Soon the park will be too hot for its namesake trees to grow. The changing climate has already brought **droughts** and caused springs to dry up. Without these water sources, animals struggle to survive.

Wildfires are another threat to the life in the park. Fires that burn through areas of the desert kill the plants. Most of the **native** plants do not regrow. New **invasive species** take their place. These new plants may not fit in the ecosystem as well.

Park staff are taking many steps to protect Joshua Tree. Soon, all park buildings will run on solar power. Park vehicles will run on electricity instead of gasoline. Workers are protecting places where Joshua trees will still be able to grow even after temperatures rise. They remove invasive plants to allow native plants to grow.

You can help protect Joshua Tree, too! Conserving water can help prevent droughts. Turning off lights and electronics when you are not using them can use less energy to reduce climate change. We can work together to keep Joshua Tree beautiful!

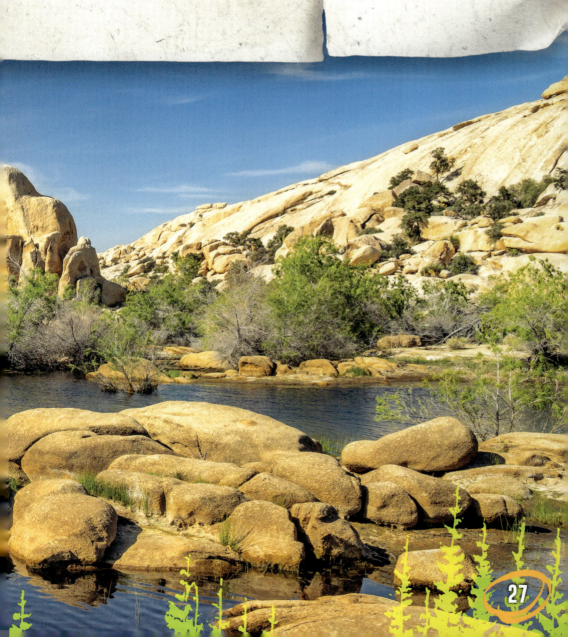

JOSHUA TREE NATIONAL PARK FACTS

Area: **1,242** square miles
(3,217 square kilometers)

Area Rank: **15TH** largest park

Date Established:
August 10, 1936
(as a national monument)

October 31, 1994
(as a national park)

Annual Visitors:
3,058,294 in 2022

Population Rank: **8TH**
most visited park in 2022

Highest Point:
Quail Mountain;
5,816 feet (1,773 meters)

TIMELINE

1848
The U.S. gains control of the land that will become Joshua Tree

1863
Smallpox devastates many Native American communities in the area

FOOD WEB

BOBCAT

RINGTAIL

BLACK-TAILED JACKRABBIT

KANGAROO RAT

JOSHUA TREE

1894
The Lost Horse Mine is first developed and continues to run until 1931

1936
President Franklin D. Roosevelt creates Joshua Tree National Monument

1994
Joshua Tree becomes a national park

GLOSSARY

canyon—a deep and narrow valley with steep sides

climate change—a human-caused change in Earth's weather due to warming temperatures

droughts—periods with little water

ecosystems—communities of living things that include plants, animals, and the environments around them

elevations—heights above sea level

erosion—the process by which rocks are worn away by wind, water, and ice

invasive species—plants or animals that are not originally from the area; invasive species often cause harm to their new environments.

magma—melted rock within the earth

native—originally from the area or having begun in the area

oasis—a green area in the desert that can support growth; oases are more than one oasis.

phenomenon—a rare or important fact or event

Pinto Culture—ancient people who lived in the area that is now Joshua Tree around 4,000 to 8,000 years ago

rain shadow desert—a desert that is formed by a mountain range blocking rainfall

resources—sources of supply or support

washes—dry areas where water has flowed

TO LEARN MORE

AT THE LIBRARY

Oachs, Emily Rose. *California*. Minneapolis, Minn.: Bellwether Media, 2022.

Payne, Stefanie. *The National Parks: Discover All 62 Parks of the United States*. New York, N.Y.: DK Publishing, 2020.

Shepherd, Jodie. *Joshua Tree*. New York, N.Y.: Children's Press, 2019.

ON THE WEB

FACTSURFER

Factsurfer.com gives you a safe, fun way to find more information.

1. Go to www.factsurfer.com.

2. Enter "Joshua Tree National Park" into the search box and click 🔍.

3. Select your book cover to see a list of related content.

INDEX

activities, 22–23
average temperatures, 11
Cahuilla, 17, 21
California, 6, 18
Chemehuevi, 17, 18, 21
climate, 8, 11, 14, 15, 24, 26, 27
climate change, 24, 27
Coachella Valley Music and Arts Festival, 21
Colorado Desert, 6, 10
fast facts, 28–29
history, 7, 9, 13, 16, 17, 18, 19, 20
Hoyt, Minerva, 20
invasive species, 24, 26
Joshua Tree National Monument, 20
Keys Ranch, 19
landscape, 4, 5, 6, 8, 9, 10, 11, 12, 14, 15, 18, 20, 22, 23, 24
location, 6
Lost Palms Oasis Trail, 4–5
map, 6
Mojave, 17
Mojave Desert, 6, 9, 10, 12
Night Sky Festival, 23
Pacific Ocean, 6, 8
Palm Springs, 6
people, 4, 5, 7, 16, 17, 18, 19, 20, 21, 22, 23, 26, 27
Pinto Culture, 16
plants, 4, 5, 6, 7, 10, 12, 13, 14, 15, 16, 18, 23, 24, 26
protecting the park, 20, 26, 27
rain shadow desert, 8
Roosevelt, Franklin D., 20
Serrano, 17, 18, 21
size, 6
Sonoran Desert, 10
threats, 24
top sites, 23
Transverse Ranges, 8
wildlife, 4, 5, 6, 12, 13, 14, 15, 16, 22, 24

The images in this book are reproduced through the courtesy of: yongyuan, front cover; William Silver, p. 3; ivanpotapoff, p. 4; Chris Curtis, p. 4 (bighorn sheep); cb_travel, pp. 4-5, 24; JaimePorElMundo, pp. 6-7; S.Vorisov, p. 9; Emily Marie Wilson, p. 10 (juniper); Jeff Whyte, p. 10; Tom Winderknecht, p. 11; Melina Fawver, p. 12 (jackrabbit, kangaroo rat); Dominic Gentilcore PhD, p. 12 (oriole); Swaroop Pixs, p. 12 (kit fox); Mat Jeppson, pp. 12 (desert night lizard), 15 (red-spotted toad); Romania Lee, p. 13 (Joshua tree); Mattia Cioni, p. 14 (cholla cactus); Brian Lasenby, p. 14 (desert horned lizard); Kelly vanDellen, pp. 15 (Mojave asters), 29 (Joshua tree); NayaDadara, pp. 16-17; History and Art Collection/ Alamy, p. 18; Doug Dolde, pp. 18-19; Steve Cukrov, p. 19 (Keys Ranch); Pictorial Press Ltd/ Alamy, p. 20 (Minerva Hoyt); MightyPix, p. 20; blazg, p. 21; Greg Epperson, p. 22 (rock climbing); Harrison Weinberg, p. 22 (camping); Light and Vision, p. 22 (Cholla Cactus Garden); Bill Florence, p. 23 (Keys Ranch); Bdingman, p. 23 (Lost Horse Mine); Squadel, p. 23 (Skull Rock); J Marshall - Tribaleye Images/ Alamy, pp. 24-25; HannaTor, pp. 26-27; maxt2274, p. 28 (1848); C. C. Pierce/ Wikipedia, p. 28 (1863); Ciar/ Wikipedia, p. 29 (1894); Leon Perskie/ Wikipedia, p. 29 (1936); Virrage Images, p. 29 (1994); Don Mammoser, p. 29 (bobcat); Carlos R Cedillo, p. 29 (ringtail); J Curtis, p. 29 (jackrabbit); Been there YB, p. 29 (kangaroo rat).